COWBOYS

Volume 4

Tales of the Wild West Series

Rick Steber

Illustrations by Don Gray

NOTE
Cowboys is the fourth book in the
Tales of the Wild West Series.

Cowboys
Volume 4
Tales of the Wild West Series

All rights reserved.
Copyright © 1988 by Rick Steber
Illustrations Copyright © 1988 by Don Gray
ISBN 0-945134-04-5

Bonanza Publishing
Box 204
Prineville, Oregon 97754

INTRODUCTION

The men who ride the open range of the far West are known under a variety of names: vaquero, range rider, mustanger and buckaroo; but the name most commonly known is cowboy.

The nature of a cowboy's work demands independence and toughness. He is a man of action; yet the long, lonely hours spent in the saddle provide ample time to develop a unique outlook on life. Simply put, a cowboy's tenet is, "What cannot be cured is endured." And endured with cheerfulness and good humor. It is far better to joke about the droughts, windstorms, blizzards, outlaw mustangs and loco cattle than to complain.

The cowboy would never have existed without his horse. Like the cowboy, the horse is referred to by an assortment of names: mustang, bronco, cayuse and, sometimes, jughead, broomtail, nag, hay burner, plug and other even less complimentary epithets. The ancestors of the western horse date back to the animals brought to America by Cortez and the conquistadores. As the Spanish mounts escaped, were lost or stolen, the horse began its phenomenal spread across western North America.

The high desert was first settled by daring stockmen who drove in foundation herds, numbering in the thousands. The cattle thrived on the native grasses and when the steers were ready for market, cowboys on horseback drove them to railroad towns in the Midwest.

With the invention of barbed wire in 1874 and an influx of homesteaders who claimed waterholes and divided up the range, the heyday of the big outfits and their cowboys passed into history. But as long as there is open sky, rimrock, bunch grass, sagebrush and juniper, cowboys will still ride the range.

FIRST CATTLE DRIVE

The first farm animals introduced to the Oregon Country were hogs and sheep brought on the ship *Tonquin* by the Astor party in 1811; later the Hudson's Bay Company shipped in a few head of cattle. The first real cattle herd in the Northwest was driven overland by mountain man Ewing Young.

In the fall of 1837 Young founded the Willamette Cattle Company, appointed himself president and led nine Willamette Valley settlers south. None had experience herding stock.

Near San Francisco Bay, Young began purchasing cattle. He paid three dollars a head until his funds were exhausted then turned the herd, numbering 800 head, north. The Spanish long-horned cattle were difficult to handle and before the drive could begin they had to be denied water and starved into submission.

Rivers posed the greatest danger and at the San Joaquin crossing, the cattle refused to go into the water. Young and the cowboys crowded the balky animals but they didn't budge. The crossing was made only after the cattle were lassoed and dragged across one by one. The process took a full week and nearly 100 animals were drowned.

The drive continued north, over the imposing Siskiyou mountain range and eventually to the Willamette Valley. The cattle that survived numbered 632 head. The drovers were paid off in cattle, Young kept a herd and the remainder were sold for an average of $7.67 a head. Young became the wealthiest man in the Oregon Country.

The herd was allowed to run wild into the foothills and it multiplied. Years later, after Young's death, descendants of the original band became troublesome to settlers, chasing and frightening their women and children. They were hunted and slaughtered for the meat.

TEXAS CATTLE

Con Shea drifted down from Canada, worked for a while as a blacksmith in the Owyhee mines before being approached by a group of moneyed men -- some say one of the madams of a Silver City house also was involved -- to trail the first herd of longhorn cattle from Texas to the Oregon Country.

Con, his brothers Jerry and Tim, and a small group of cowboys traveled to Texas where they put together a herd of 1,000 head. They drove them north to Kansas over established cattle trails and sometimes blazing their own, then swung west over the route of the Oregon Trail.

Con rode ahead to locate water and grass for noon camp while the cowboys moved the cattle: two on point -- one on each side, two in the swing, two in the flank and the rest bringing up the drag. At the end of the day the cattle were allowed to graze at the bed ground. The theory was if they were full they would not cause trouble during the hours of darkness. Guards were posted through the night, two riders at a time circling the herd, singing to them, keeping them quiet and content.

Con and his men completed the 2,000-mile drive late in the fall of 1867, delivered the cattle and turned around to build another herd of Texas longhorns. This time they profited from the experience of the first drive and purchased, at a low price, some steers and cows of poor quality.

As they passed through sections of the trail, Indian tribes would meet them as they did the wagon trains and demand payment for crossing their lands. Con would negotiate a payment and give a number of the poorer trading cattle. This way they were able to save the better animals.

Another thing that made the second drive more profitable, and faster, was that Con refused to purchase cows with calves. If a calf was born on the drive, its throat was cut. That way a mother was never slowed by her offspring.

3

THE TIGHT CINCH

Many of the early-day cattle drives from the Oregon Country to midwestern markets passed through Miles City, Montana. A lady who grew up near there remembered as a child watching huge herds of longhorn cattle being driven across the Yellowstone River.

"One herd arrived when the river was bank full and dangerous looking," she recalled. "The cowboys began preparing for the crossing. Each man loosened his saddle cinch except one young chap who had never ridden in swimming water. He tightened his -- just another case of thinking the little things in life don't count.

"The herd was crowded off the bank into the treacherous stream. When part way over the leaders tried to double back, forming a mill. Bill Case, one of the old hands, seemed to be everywhere trying to break the mill and encouraging the other cowboys when someone shouted, 'The kid's gone down.' Case managed to get to where the kid was last seen and when his head appeared above water, he yelled at him to grab a steer's tail. About then the silent, churning animals took action and made for shore.

"Case shouted at the boy to swim high and that kid was bouncing high when that old steer started up the other side. He looked like the weight on a kite's tail. As the steer made for the cottonwood trees the kid let loose and, to avoid the herd's hooves that were cracking over the stones, he shinnied up a tree. Dripping wet but happy, the kid dropped on the horse of the first rider to reach him.

"His plucky horse had swum until the tightened cinch cut off his wind. It drifted down, coming out on the opposite shore. That little pony had filled with water; his ears were hanging way down until he looked about like a German dachshund."

4

LIFE OF A BUCKAROO

John Loggan was a high desert buckaroo. Recalling the vitality of his experiences he said, "I worked on the P Ranch in 1892. There were fifteen or twenty men at headquarters and about the same number who rode the range.

"The next spring I worked for the White Horse Ranch. The grass was so bountiful that only cows with calves and the heifers were fed hay during the winter months. In the last days of March or early April the cattle would be driven out to the range. After that we would start to round up the horses and brand the colts. Following this it was time to start after the cattle, to round them up and mark and brand the calves.

"On these roundups there would be fifteen or twenty men in the crew, men representing outfits who drifted cattle on the range. A chuck wagon would follow along. As there were few corrals, all the marking and branding was done by roping and dragging calves to the fire.

"In the fall it was roundup time again to get the market steers. They were driven to Winnemucca, Nevada, in bunches of about 1,000 in a drive. It was 135 miles and took from eight to ten days.

"One time I was sent on a trip to Denio and on the way called on the Catlow family, for whom the Catlow Valley was named. I was greeted by Mrs. John Catlow, an English woman. The ranch house was made of rough boards on the outside but was very neat and artistically arranged on the inside. I was greatly astonished to look on a life-sized painting of Mrs. Catlow. Talking with her she informed me that it had cost $5,000 to have it painted. That seemed like a terrible lot of money to a buckaroo drawing board and room and $35 a month."

5

MYSTERY MAN

He stood on the front porch of the ranch house, hat in hand, boyishly handsome. In an eastern accent he asked for employment, saying, "I know very little about ranch work but I am willing to learn."

"What's your name?" the rancher wanted to know.

"Slim."

"That's it? Just Slim?" questioned the rancher.

"Just Slim," came the reply.

The rancher gave the boy a job. And in return Slim worked hard. He was quiet, never volunteered personal information and skillfully avoided all questions relating to where he was from or how he happened to come to this remote corner of the West. For six years Slim stayed at the ranch learning to ride, rope and work cattle. On weekends when the other cowboys journeyed to town Slim never accompanied them. He stayed behind, in the bunkhouse. Six years. And then one day, while the other ranch hands were eating dinner, Slim pushed his chair back from the table. He walked across the room and took a seat on the piano bench. He did not glance down but it was quickly evident he was intimately knowledgeable of the keyboard.

He stared out the window at the rounded hills and the skyline broken by sagebrush and juniper while his fingers traced through a series of fluid notes, then launched into a haunting melody that came from deep in the soul of the quiet young man. The music boomed like thunder through the mountains and slowly faded to little more than wind turning aspen leaves. And Slim, shoulders bent and head bowed, cried like a long lost child.

Suddenly he stopped. He wiped at his eyes with the heels of his hands, addressed the cowboys staring at him with, "I'm sorry. Guess I forgot where I was," and quickly left the room.

The following day Slim drew his wages and departed the ranch. No one out west heard from him again.

INDIAN HORSEMEN

The Nez Perce Indians were some of the best horsemen in the West. They rode a special breed of horse -- the Appaloosa -- which they developed.

The nature of the Nez Perce was to accept no weakness in man or beast. They rode their horses hard and required them to range for feed. Only the hardiest survived. Selective breeding was practiced by killing inferior colts.

The unique horse was large-bodied. It had big lungs and great stamina as well as speed. Its front legs were close together, making him surefooted on narrow trails and over rough terrain. But the most noticeable thing about the Appaloosa was its peculiar spotted rump.

The Appaloosa brought the Nez Perce respect and riches. It was used as a war horse against neighboring tribes and was a choice trade item. Gatherings at Celilo Falls always saw the Appaloosa bring high returns in exchange for smoked salmon, berries, Indian tobacco and sea shells.

When the Nez Perce crossed the Rocky Mountains to hunt buffalo, their spotted ponies were eagerly sought by the Crow, Sioux, and Arapaho. The Nez Perce made it a practice to trade only the poorest horses, thereby guarding their breeding stock. Lewis and Clark reported the Nez Perce were expert horsemen and that the Appaloosa was superior to any other bloodline. After the explorers came fur traders and then pioneers swept into the country. They wanted the Indian land. The Nez Perce were forced into fighting and the United States Army chased the band 1,300 miles before cornering them in the Bear Paw Mountains of Montana.

For many years after the Bear Paw massacre any Appaloosa on the open range was liable to be shot on sight because it was a symbol of the Nez Perce. A few horses in scattered locations survived and are the foundation stock of the popular Appaloosa breed of today.

SCARED

Rancher Henry Davidson was talking to a cattle buyer and by chance happened to mention an incident that occurred many years before.

"I'd just sold a herd of cattle and was carrying $10,000 in gold," Henry told. "At the going rate that came to nearly fifty pounds. It was packed in a leather case.

"I had passage on a steamboat. We came up as far as Corvallis and laid over, so I put up at a hotel. We were scheduled to leave early the next morning.

"I remember getting up in the dark and going outside. The day looked gloomy, it was raining. And as I walked toward the landing I got this tight feeling in the pit of my stomach. I knew something dreadful was about to happen.

"My hollow footsteps on the boardwalk reminded me how alone and vulnerable I was with my gold. And then I heard faint footfalls echoing my own. I walked quietly, listening. The footfalls were coming from behind me. I sped up. They sped up.

"The steamboat blew its whistle. I stole a peek over my shoulder but it was too dark to see. All the while every bad scenario in the book came to mind. The man behind me had a gun. He was going to knock me in the head and steal my gold. He was going to shoot me.

"I started to run. Behind me, over my own racing heart, I heard him running. At one point the handle ripped from my case but I caught it in midair and never stopped running until I was safely on board the steamboat.

"Yes sir, that's about as scared as I have ever been."

The cattle buyer laughed until he had tears in his eyes. When he could find the words he told Henry he was the other man. He had been carrying gold to buy cattle and had heard footsteps on the boardwalk. When the steamboat blew its whistle and the footsteps he had been listening to started running, he became scared and started running, too.

9

TAYLOR GRAZING

The open range existed for three-quarters of a century. Horses, cattle and sheep competed for available grasses; they over-grazed the open range to such an extent that it was nearly destroyed.

Some men traveled through the West allowing their stock to graze off the public domain. The legitimate land-owning ranchers resented these drifting operators and called the cattlemen "rawhiders" and the sheepmen "tramps". At first the ranchers banded together into associations, trying to scare the drifters into grazing somewhere else. When this tactic failed, they resorted to violence. Guns blazed.

By the 1930s cooler heads had prevailed and ranchers were working toward a federal law that would protect their interests. As a result, the Taylor Grazing Act became law in 1934. It required all users of the public range to prove they had a base of operations. Rawhiders and tramps were forced out and risked stiff fines and confiscation of their livestock if they defied the law.

The remaining operators were ranked according to the number of years each outfit had been using the range. The Bureau of Land Management (BLM) began interpreting, administering and enforcing the law, trying to turn the tide on decades of range abuse.

At first the ranchers were pleased but in time they came to detest the aggressiveness of the BLM in restricting their use of the land. Lawsuits were filed and even when ranchers won in court they still lost from the high costs of attorney fees. The BLM had the treasury of the United States behind it.

The Taylor Grazing Act effectively broke up the big ranches of the West, spelling doom to the free-wheeling life of the outfit cowboy.

HANK VAUGHN

Hank Vaughn was a rogue buckaroo, quick on the draw and a mean customer when he was drinking. He is credited within his lifetime of collecting 13 slugs.

One time Hank was sitting in a saloon in eastern Oregon drinking whiskey. A stranger came through the swinging doors and Hank ordered him to dance. When the man did not dance fast enough Hank drew his revolver and emptied it into the floor. The stranger got even. A few days later he slipped up on Hank and wounded him in the right arm. While Hank was recuperating he tacked playing cards to the wall of his room and practiced drawing and shooting with his left hand.

Another time Hank was drinking in a saloon in Prineville, Oregon. He got into an argument with a fellow named Charley Long and challenged his adversary to grab the corner of a bandanna. Each man took hold. The bandanna stretched tight, they drew and fired. When the smoke cleared both men lay on the floor. Hank survived.

Hank's courage was limitless. One time a train Hank was riding as a passenger was stopped by robbers. Hank pulled a gun and disposed of the outlaws. Laws did not bind him and he once did a stretch in jail for rustling horses.

The stormy life of Hank Vaughn ended at age 46. That day he was drinking and running his horse through the streets of Pendleton. His horse threw him and he fell headlong into a pile of rocks.

But even in death the wild times continued. At his funeral a runaway destroyed a hack in the procession and seven men were injured.

YOUNGEST COWBOY

Eight-year-old Gibby Masterson was up early, dressed and wearing his brand new red boots. This was the day his father had promised he could help with branding.

Gibby was halfway to the barn before the screen door slammed shut. He hung on behind his father as they rode to the pasture where Gibby tended the fire while the cowboys roped calves and dragged them bawling and kicking toward the branding area. He was Johnny-on-the-spot every time the men called for the iron.

About mid-morning one of the cowboys rode in leading a horse. "This is my spare," he told Gibby. "I won't be needin' 'im. You can have 'im for the day if you don't mind ridin' bareback." He gave Gibby a hand up and the boy was bursting with pride as he rode to where the cowboys were working. He was one of them, helping cut out the calves to be branded.

Finally someone hollered, "Dinner time." The cowboys turned their mounts toward the barn in a slow gallop. Gibby followed. But as his horse leaped a small ditch he lost his balance. There was no saddle horn to grab so he could not right himself. Gibby fell, hit the ground, bounced and lay there in the scrubby sage momentarily stunned, the wind knocked out of him. When he did manage to draw a breath he was crying.

One of the cowboys happened to witness the fall. He caught the horse and led him to where Gibby lay. "That was a heck of a ride," he told the boy. "I saw the way he was buckin'. I don't know how you stayed with him as long as you did."

After the initial shock it had been mostly Gibby's dignity that had suffered. The cowboy's remarks soothed that hurt. Gibby quit crying, wiped his eyes and after a helping hand up, he rode on in for some of his mother's fine cooking.

HORSE TRADING

This is the story of an outlaw horse taken off the high desert by a mustanger and traded to a greenhorn attorney in the town of La Grande, Oregon.

"I can ride this little pony. No problem," announced the attorney. He tied the horse to an awning post in front of his main street office. Paying two men to hold the horse's head, he went about the process of saddling. The lawyer was new to town and word of the transaction had spread. A fair-sized crowd had gathered to watch the fun by the time he pulled the slack from the cinch strap.

The attorney made sure his freshly-brushed Stetson was snug before swinging into the saddle. The two men holding the mustang's head stepped back.

The horse stood absolutely still, ears laid flat, eyes showing white. It appeared he would explode at any instant but the point of detonation seemed never to occur. Except for the nostrils alternately flaring and closing and the sound of air rushing to be drawn and expelled, the scene could have been a photograph. Seconds stretched and warped. Finally a few in the crowd began to snicker and laugh.

"This pony's broke," called out the attorney. "Untie me!" Hands reached for the rope tied around the awning post. It was at that instant the fuse reached powder.

The mustang humped his back like a mule in a hailstorm and commenced bucking. The attorney grabbed at leather needlessly as he was tossed over the horse's head and landed roughly on the boardwalk spread-eagled, his trousers ripped open and his hindside exposed.

As an added indignity the bronc wheeled, taking the awning post with him. The awning came down on the greenhorn attorney and when he managed to crawl out from under it, his head was sticking through the crown of his cowboy hat.

13

FOUND DEAD HERE

A cowboy found a horse standing by a fence line, saddle turned under its belly and a lasso around its neck which had obviously been cut. The saddle was recognized as belonging to Jack Frusetta, a cowboy who worked for the SL Ranch, an outfit headquartered in Elko, Nevada.

Word was spread and working men from neighboring ranches launched a search. The last anyone had heard from Jack was that he was trailing a small bunch of cattle off the range near where the states of Nevada, Idaho and Oregon meet. Within a few days Jack's pack horse was found with the lead rope wedged in a clump of sagebrush. The animal was in terrible condition suffering from lack of feed and water.

The cowboys spread out and searched the high plain. After several hours one of the men fired his pistol, signaling the others. They converged to find evidence, a sagebrush fire and Jack's bullwhip. He was a hand with a bullwhip and it was evident he had used the whip to cut and pull chunks of sagebrush to him.

Every indication was that Jack had been seriously injured. They found where the saddle horse's lead rope had been tied. The consensus was that Jack had either broken his back or his legs and could not mount. Lending credence to the theory was the trail they found where Jack had drug himself through the snow and mud.

They traveled three miles, locating the remains of 19 small fires, before finding Jack. He was lying on his back, hat tipped as if to provide shading from the sun and gloves neatly folded and laid with spurs beside him. How he must have suffered those last days with a dislocated hip, and no food, water or shelter from the harsh environment!

The cowboys drove a pipe into the ground to mark the spot. A plaque was added later. Its message was direct, "In memory of Jack Frusetta, found dead here."

SEVEN WHITE HORSES

At the turn of the century there were seven white horses that roamed the high desert between Summer Lake and Lakeview, Oregon.

Visitors to the area were always impressed by their first sight of the seven, running single file through the sage, manes and tails blowing in the wind. They almost appeared to be phantoms.

Whenever a newcomer commented about seeing the horses, the locals would act extremely interested and relate stories about a reward for their capture. Sometimes they would say it was a wealthy eastern gentleman offering several thousand dollars because he wanted the horses to pull his hearse when he died. Sometimes they would say it was a California movie producer wanting the seven to star in a motion picture.

Eventually the truth would be related. The horses, all geldings, were branded with the Circle-on-the-Jaw brand and belonged to a rancher at Summer Lake. The rancher had tried numerous times to catch the horses but always failed.

One spring cowboys were surprised to see a roan horse running with the seven. After that the roan was always with the little band. And it was the roan that eventually cost the horses their freedom.

Reub Long, a well-known high desert buckaroo, purchased the Circle-on-the-Jaw brand. He tricked the roan into coming in to a water hole. The others followed and were captured.

Never again did the seven white horses run free and wild through the painted hills and across the open flats. They became only a memory, a fading memory that will die with the passing of the last of the old high-desert cowboys.

MULES

Oswald West visited Klamath Falls the summer of 1905 and reported: "I found myself in that town on business connected with the State Land Office. While taking an after-dinner stroll along the main street I was to witness what, to me, was a distressing performance.

"A couple of cowhands, well-liquored up, were exhibiting an undersized, half-broken, foot-sore team of mules hitched to a top buggy. They would race them up and down the street to demonstrate how quickly they could be stopped in front of a saloon where drinks would be ordered.

"Seeing that the abused animals needed a friend I made inquiries as to whether they were for sale. Being told that the outfit was for sale for $150 I informed the gentlemen I was not interested in the buggy and harness, only the mules. The deal, therefore, appeared to be off.

"Along about one o'clock in the morning I was awakened by a loud knock at my hotel room door. 'Are you the guy who wanted to buy our mules?' I was asked. We struck a deal for $90, on the condition I pay them $10 in advance. They badly needed whiskey money.

"In the morning, unfortunately, I discovered the mules had not been broken to ride. This necessitated my hiring a saddle nag. The only one available was somewhat advanced in years, stiff in the shoulders and unshod. An old hornless stock saddle supplied was quite in keeping with the horse.

"I rode this animal to within about 15 miles of Ashland before it became foot-sore and weary. So I removed the saddle and bridle and hiked on, leading my two mules."

The mules were shipped by train from Ashland to Salem. They were turned out to pasture and were never worked again. Oswald West went on to become the 14th governor of the State of Oregon.

COWBOY DOCTOR

Dr. Marsden was the "cowboy doctor". He would go anywhere within several hundred square miles of his hometown Burns, Oregon to treat a sick or injured cowboy.

Denny O'Brien drove for Dr. Marsden in 1897 and 1898. He wrote, "One time I held a light for him while he took a piece of bone out of Ira Mahon's fractured skull and put in a silver plate. A horse had thrown Ira and bashed in his head.

"Doc had an only brother George who was bookkeeper at the P Ranch. When he suddenly became ill they sent for the doctor. We got there at 1 a.m. and George was already dead. Doc asked them to lift the sheet off his brother's face and as he stood there looking down at that dead face I could see the cords in his neck swell. Poor Doc -- he took it hard. Later on I drove him back to Burns and, as he was worn out, he fell asleep in the rig.

"It was so cold and my hands hurt me terrible, but after I changed teams at the Narrows they didn't hurt me anymore. When we drove into Burns it was 42 degrees below zero. I made sure Doc was taken care of and then I stumbled into Broady Johnson's saloon and started for the stove. Broady told me, 'Stay away from the stove or you'll lose your hands if you do.' He cut off my gloves -- my hands were white as chalk halfway to my elbows -- and sent one of his customers to fetch a pan of coal oil and another of snow.

"Broady rubbed my hands first with snow, then in the coal oil. Not until about four in the morning did the circulation begin to come into them. And I have no words to tell you how those hands ached. I wouldn't send for the doctor. He was all worn out and had just lost his only brother.

"Well, the next morning my hands were as black as coal and the skin peeled all off and, oh, the intolerable aching. I never held a rein again for six weeks but old Broady, God bless him, he saved my hands. My hands still bother me in cold weather and I suppose they always will."

18

LAST CATTLE DRIVE

One of the last big cattle drives in Oregon got underway in February 1926. Buckaroo Harold Baker recalled, "We had run out of feed and the outfit boss, Seth Dixon, said to drive the herd from where we were holding them on the Upper Crooked River to Bend. From there they would be shipped by rail to Klamath Falls where Seth had extra hay.

"There were seven of us, counting the cook, trailing 2,150 head of two- and three-year-old steers. The morning we pulled out it turned cold and stormy. The first night we had ten inches of wet snow drop on us and it was miserable. Took seven days and the last couple we had a steady stream of newspaper reporters and ordinary citizens coming to take pictures. They thought it was a pretty big deal.

"We reached Bend and extra police had to be put on to keep the crowd back so we could get the cattle to the stockyard. Just as the leaders were reaching their destination an engine let off steam, spooked the animals and they stampeded, ran about a half mile before we could turn them.

"There were two small corrals at the stockyard which would hold about a carload apiece. We had to keep the herd in the street, drive a little bunch into the corral, load them into a car and do it all over again.

"We rode the train with the cattle and unloaded them in Klamath Falls. Seth was so pleased with the job we had done that he treated the lot of us to supper at the fanciest restaurant in town. The tables had white tablecloths and more silverware than we could have used in a week.

"Having spent eight days in wet weather driving cattle, loading and unloading them, we were pretty rank smelling, I'm sure. There were some ladies at a nearby table that kept acting like they were about to faint. And the waiters didn't much want to wait on us until Seth loosened the purse strings and let it be known he was willing to spend good money."

19

BIG ED

Cigarette smoke hung like a ground fog in the crowded saloon. Cowboys stood belly to the bar, throwing back their heads, tossing down drinks. All of a sudden the swinging doors were flung open and a high-pitched voice barked over the din, "Big Ed's comin'!"

Patrons scattered in every direction, leaving behind only the bartender. Within a few minutes there was the sound of a great whirlwind outside, one section of the wall collapsed inward and a huge, red-bearded man riding a ten-foot tall polar bear and using a logging chain for reins and a live rattlesnake for a whip rode in and dismounted. He hollered, "Give me a drink!" and the building shook like a toothpick house in a gale.

The bartender nervously set a bottle of whiskey on the bar, slid it toward the stranger and returned to cower in the far corner. The stranger grabbed it in his fist, drank it all in one tremendous gulp and then chewed the bottle and swallowed it.

"Sir, would ... would you care for another?" stuttered the timid bartender.

The big man shook his head, muttered, "Naw," and remounted the polar bear. Just before he swung the rattlesnake whip, he called to the bartender, "Don't have time for another drink. Ain't you heard? Big Ed's comin'."

20

THE MILK COW

The high desert was open range for the big horse and cattle outfits, until homesteaders arrived to string barbed wire around land they claimed as their own.

The Homestead Law of 1862 entitled any citizen of the United States to acquire 160 acres of the public domain, provided he lived on the property for five years. In 1877 the Desert Land Act allowed homesteaders to claim 320 acres if they irrigated it.

One story about an early homesteader was told by John Hailey who operated a freight wagon over The Dalles military road. "Was down to Rock Creek crossin'," he told friends. "Feller name of Butler settled there on a homestead couple years back. Had himself quite a pile of meadow hay. Stopped to see if I could buy a little fer my team. Butler said, 'Naw, can't spare none, need it for my own stock.'

"Well now, I knew he hadn't come in there with much an' I mentioned the fact. He agreed, said, 'When I took my claim I only had one yoke of steers and an ol' milk cow. But by careful management I now have 35 head, mostly calves an' yearlings.'

"I scratched my head. It was pretty evident he had been helpin' himself to calves on the open range but a man doesn't want to just come right out and call someone a cattle rustler, so I tell him, 'Mr. Butler, you got yourself a special milk cow.' And I ask, 'How much will you take fer her?' Of course, he wouldn't sell."

21

THE LAST ROUNDUP

One of the last great horse roundups off the open range was accomplished in the spring of 1947 by pilots Lonnie Shurtleff, Bill Antone and rancher Rankin Crow and his cowboys.

Planes were used to herd wild mustangs to a drift fence and down to a holding corral where two cowboys jumped from hiding places and ran together, tying off a rope gate. Feed sacks were strung from the rope and once a horse was inside the enclosure it would rarely escape.

One big gray stud refused to allow his little band of mares to be herded into the trap. Every time they were pushed toward the corral he veered them away. The pilots tried to turn him, first by using the shadow of the plane to cross in front and then by dropping bags of lime that hit the ground in an explosion of white dust.

Bill Antone told Rankin, "I'm gonna get that son of a buck if it's the last thing I do. I was shot down over Germany. I'm not afraid."

The following day, when the stud tried to turn back, Bill was there. He swooped so low that the wheel of his plane hit the rump of the horse and he went rolling end over end. The plane circled, came back around and passed over the cowboys. Bill dipped his wings side to side and proceeded to drive the gray's mares toward the trap.

A total 647 horses were rounded up and loaded into trucks. They were a wild bunch, fought the loading and the drive to the railhead at Juntura with every ounce of strength they possessed. Afterwards Rankin commented, "All the truckers could do was go like hell and hope for the best."

22

THE BELL

Island Ranch south of Burns, Oregon was the northern headquarters of the far-flung Miller & Lux cattle outfit.

In the fall cowboys gathered well-fed steers off the open range for the trail drive to the railhead in Winnemucca, Nevada. They always looked forward to reaching town where they would enjoy the taste of liquor and the company of women.

One year was trouble from the start when the cattle wanted to double back to the lush swamp grass surrounding headquarters. The cowboys worked the whole drive, sweating and cursing, to keep the cattle lined out and heading south through the high desert.

After two weeks of fighting cattle they broke over the last dividing ridge. There below was the Humboldt River, winding lazily back and forth across the floor of the valley. The cattle smelled water, snorted, threw their heads in the air and broke into a trot. Once their thirst was quenched the cowboys drove them on toward the railroad stockyard. As they eased up the street one of the cowboys rode ahead to open the gate.

At this critical point a steam engine puffed down the track, bell ringing. The steers stampeded. For the remainder of that day the Miller & Lux cowboys roped and pulled steers from backyards and alleyways. They worked until dark. Then they put up their horses and retired to the nearest saloon. Spirits flowed like spring water.

Late that night, as they grumbled about their extra work, one of the men suggested, "We ought to find that engine and take the bell so other cowboys won't have to suffer."

That was all it took. The men tossed money on the bar, took bottles with them and started for the railyard.

When they turned toward home the next day they had the bell with them. It still hangs from the roof of the main house at Island Ranch and three times a day, for breakfast, dinner and supper, it rings.

24

FIRECRACKER

A buckaroo met Rankin Crow and Harold Johnson as they rode into the Alvord ranch headquarters. He said to them, "You fellers are pretty fair hands. Thought you might be able to help. We've got a horse. Every time we hitch him up, he lays down. Know anything we can do to cure that?"

"Yep," replied Rankin. He ordered the problem horse hitched to a hay wagon alongside a gentle horse. And while this was being done Rankin dug into his bedroll, took out a firecracker and slipped it into his pocket.

"You drive," Rankin directed his companion. The horses were hitched. Harold crawled up on the seat and gathered the reins. It was at that point that the problem horse, a bay, lay down with a groan.

Rankin went to the bay, petted and talked to it. "Tried that approach," said the buckaroo, but Rankin ignored the remark, rubbed the horse in its sensitive spot behind the ears, stroked its neck and patted its back. He withdrew the firecracker and, making sure he kept his body between the back of the horse and the men, he slipped the firecracker under the tail of the bay. He managed to light the fuse without being seen and stepped back.

The firecracker exploded with a sharp bang and the bay leaped to his feet kicking, bucking, and took off running across the desert, the other horse running to keep up.

On the original jolt Harold, who had been standing, was knocked over backwards into the wagon bed. He was thrown around unmercifully as the bouncing wagon struck clumps of sagebrush and exposed rocks. But finally Harold was able to gain his feet. He crawled back onto the seat, caught a flying rein and slowly achieved control. At last the horses stood, sides heaving. Harold allowed them a short blow before turning around.

Ever after the bay, which turned out to be a hard worker, was called Firecracker.

25

THE JUMP

A pair of rustlers was making a sweep of the high desert stealing everything not tied down. They had 70 head of horses, many with pack saddles loaded with plunder, when they were overtaken by a posse of irate settlers from the Umatilla area.

The rustlers cut loose the pack animals and in the ensuing confusion they escaped, heading for high ground into the foothills of the Blue Mountains. Unfamiliar with the lay of the land they turned up a canyon which dead-ended into a steep rock bluff. They might climb out but they would never ride out. The posse sealed off the entrance. The thieves were trapped.

"Lay down your guns. Come out with your hands over your heads," was the order. In response came the whine of ricochetting metal and the sharp crack of a rifle. For the next hour the two sides exchanged gunfire. And then it abruptly ceased. All was quiet except for the soft moaning of the wind through rock formations. Shadows melted together. Darkness crept over the land.

"We'll give back the horses if you let us go," called one of the rustlers. They had seven horses between them.

"No dice," called the leader of the posse, but by then the telltale sound of horses was coming down the trail. They blended into the darkness and no one noticed the outlaws riding to the side, Indian style, until it was too late. Then came surprised yells, quick shots. But the outlaws avoided the bullets and after making a short run across a sagebrush flat they went straight up the steep face of a hill, kicking loose shale on their pursuers.

At the top of the ridge the Cascades could be seen, faintly outlined against a thin grey strip of sky. Ahead was a gaping cut, a lava fissure 12 feet across and more than 100 feet deep. For the outlaws there was no turning back. They dug in their spurs and forced their mounts to jump.

The posse chose not to follow.

26

EARP

Wyatt Earp was the famous one, involved in more than 100 gun battles, marshal of Wichita, Dodge City and Tombstone and fighting on the side of law and order at the OK Corral shoot-out. Less familiar was his brother Virgil.

Virgil was a teenager when he married. The Civil War erupted and he fought on the Union side, was reported to have been killed. His wife, who by then had given birth to a daughter she named Nellie, thought herself a free woman, remarried and took Nellie to Oregon.

Virgil was seriously wounded but survived the war. Since he had no place to call home he roamed, following in his brother's footsteps. He was in Dodge City and for a few weeks was Wyatt's deputy marshal. He stood beside Wyatt at the OK Corral and took a slug in the leg. And like Wyatt he was appointed marshal of Tombstone, one of the wildest towns in existence.

The evening of October 28, 1882, Virgil made a mistake that nearly cost him his life. He allowed himself to be silhouetted and a slug slammed into his arm, shattering the bone just above the elbow. His days as a lawman and gunfighter were over.

He went to California and visited Wyatt, who had retired and gone into the real estate business, and then drifted north to Oregon to visit his daughter Nellie. During his stay in Portland a reporter for the *Oregonian* interviewed him and wrote, "Earp carries a lame arm which is plugged full of lead, and can tell many reminiscences that affect the hair like a stiff sea breeze."

When the big strike was made in Goldfield, Nevada, Virgil and Wyatt rushed there to be in on the action. Virgil died in Goldfield of natural causes on October 20, 1905. Word was sent to Nellie that if she wanted the body of her father she should come claim it. She did. And that is why the body of Virgil Earp will repose for eternity in Portland's Riverview Cemetery.

27

P RANCH HAYING

Longhorn Texas cattle were driven 2,500 miles to the Oregon Country where stockmen allowed them to range free, even in the winter. But several years of severe weather in the 1880s convinced stockmen to put up hay.

On the P Ranch, one of the West's most famous spreads, haying began in late spring. The working stock, 200 head of so-called gentle horses and another 30 head of mustangs, were rounded up and brought to headquarters.

The mustangs were corralled, roped and thrown to the ground. One by one they were taken to the big round barn, built as a horse-breaking facility by ranch owner Pete French, where they were haltered and tied short so they would not hurt themselves. They were fed but denied water. After several days even the wildest and most head-strong mustang could be led to water.

The next step in the breaking process was for the cowboys to hobble a horse and tie a back leg so that if it started fighting, the rope would come tight and the animal would be jerked off its feet.

After a mustang had lost some of its wildness and learned not to fight the restraints, it was teamed with one of the experienced horses and hitched to a bronco cart. The cart was hard pulling. The green horse would soon wear itself out and then the learning process could begin. After a few hours on the bronco cart, the mustang was ready for work.

The cowboys of the P Ranch harvested hay from the tall marsh grass surrounding Malheur Lake. The fields were immense and it would take from early morning until noon for the horse-pulled mowing machines to complete a circle. Always there were cowboys riding along, lariats in hand, waiting to rope any mustang that tried to run away.

SHOOTING OF TIL

Til Taylor was known as the "Cowboy Sheriff". He was president of the Pendleton Round-Up for nine years and was the sheriff of Umatilla County for 18 years until that fateful day, July 25, 1920, when his prisoners broke jail.

Til entered his office to find five prisoners rifling through his desk. One of the men, Owens, grabbed the sheriff and in the resulting fight Til's pistol was knocked from his holster. It was scooped up and someone called, "Shoot now!" A shot was fired. It missed.

"Shoot again." The bullet slammed into Til's chest, into his heart, and killed him instantly.

The five escaped. They caught a ride on the first freight and rode six miles to the old Umatilla Indian mission. The brakeman saw them jump.

A posse, with drawn guns and aided by bloodhounds, conducted a search of the wheatfields and the brushy draws leading into the Blue Mountains. A trail was located and followed eighteen miles to a construction camp at the base of Cabbage Hill. The meat house had been broken into.

The trail seemed to end there. It was not until four days later, after the posse had broken into small groups, that one of the groups came upon an isolated sheep camp.

A man dismounted, stepped to the tent and threw back the canvas flap. The sheepherder was in bed. The man asked him, "We're with the posse looking for the murderers of Til Taylor. Seen anyone come through?"

The sheepherder propped himself up with an elbow. And as he answered, "No, I haven't," he was pointing with his finger behind him to where two men lay on a cot. They were arrested without a fight.

That same day, a short distance away, the other fugitives were discovered and returned to Pendleton. Capital punishment had been approved by voters the year before, making it possible for the murderers of the popular Cowboy Sheriff to receive the appropriate justice.

THE RIDE

With the silent backing of Henry Miller, legendary partner of Miller & Lux cattle company, Tom Overstreet was able to pull together an outfit that encompassed much of southeastern Oregon. The crown jewel of the sprawling empire, simply referred to as "The Company", was to be the Agency Valley.

Agency Valley had been set aside as an Indian reservation. The government had tried to civilize the remnants of local tribes and make them farmers; but the Indians revolted and went on the warpath. They were hunted down by white men and killed. That left a reservation with no Indians. Henry Miller had told Overstreet, "I can never forget the Agency Valley. It is beautiful and will make a wonderful headquarters. Keep your eyes open and when it is offered for sale, buy it at any price."

The government posted the land to be sold at public auction in Lakeview, Oregon but Overstreet, working in Silvies Valley, was not notified until the day before the auction. Lakeview was 200 miles away. Overstreet leaped on his horse and began one of the greatest rides in the annals of the West.

Overstreet rode day and night, exchanging horses with riders he met, trading horses at the scattered ranches along the way. He galloped across the Warner Mountains with morning light streaking the sky.

The hands of the clock in the Lakeview land office were lined at 12 noon; the receiver was holding up the sale notice when Overstreet burst into the room. He outbid all others and claimed the valuable Agency Valley for The Company.

Shortly after making the now-famous ride, Overstreet was involved in an accident. He was riding a spirited horse when the saddle slipped. Overstreet was dragged to death. His widow sold her interest in The Company to Miller and it was merged into the vast holdings of Miller & Lux.

31

TWO TRAINS

This is the story of a train wreck. Two trains, one going east and the other west, crashed on a blind curve. All the crewmen and the passengers were killed.

A railroad investigator was dispatched to the scene to determine the cause of the accident. He discovered only one eyewitness, a range rider. He interviewed him, asking him to relate the details of the terrible collision.

"Well," he drawled, "I happened to be up there on the ridge, herdin' a maverick I picked up back in the dry wash. I was stayin' back and not pushin' too terrible hard. Pokin' along, mindin' my own business, not thinkin' 'bout much of anythin' 'cept gettin' back to the ranch 'fore it got dark an' wonderin' what the cook was gonna be fixin' fer dinner. Right about then I sure coulda used a cup of strong coffee...."

"If you don't mind, could you skip to the train wreck?" interjected the investigator.

"Sure. Well, anyway, I seen one train comin' one way and the other comin' right at 'im. I'll bet they was goin' forty miles an hour, or thereabouts. Looked to me as if they was fixin' to meet on the blind curve at the foot of the ridge."

"Did you try to warn them?"

"Naw."

"You didn't even think about trying to stop them?"

"Maybe a little."

"Just exactly what did you think?"

"I thought to myself, two trains on the same track -- now that's a hell of a way to run a railroad."

COWBOY STORY

According to this yarn, a cowboy named Slim returned to the bunkhouse after having a wild spree in town the night before. The others called greetings.

"Have a good time?" asked one with a knowing wink.

"Not too good," drawled Slim. "When I got to town I had a hundred bucks but now I'm flat broke. Not a thin dime to my name."

"What'd ya do with it?"

"I'll tell ya. First thing I did was go to the Pastime and order a shot of whiskey for myself and a round for the house. Then I ordered another. When I paid the bill it came to fifteen bucks.

"I went across the street to the A-Z and bought a round for the house there. A sweet gal named Rosy got hold of me and I couldn't of got rid of her even if I had wanted to. So I asked her if she would care to have dinner with me. We et and I bought a few more rounds. We were havin' quite a time. I paid for dinner and drinks, came to forty.

"After that we moseyed down to the Waterhole, had a few more drinks. Ended up spending twenty-five more. And now I'm flat broke."

"Hold it. That doesn't add up," claimed one of the cowboys. "You spent fifteen, forty and twenty-five. If my math's right it comes to eighty. So where did the rest of it go?"

"I don't know," said Slim, shaking his head ruefully. "I must have blown the last twenty foolishly."

GREAT EQUALIZER

The history of the West is marked by distinct eras. First was the Indian, living with nature in an unending cycle. Then came mountain men trapping the streams for beaver and other fur-bearing animals. Following them were wagon pioneers who settled the most fertile and well-watered valleys. In their wake came miners lured by the promise of striking it rich in the gold fields. As each wave washed over the West the native inhabitants were pushed from ancestral grounds onto reservations.

With the Indian population gone, the interior was opened for an influx of ranchers who recognized the great potential of the high desert. Here was a bonanza every bit as rich as beaver, farmland or gold. Ranchers laid claim to vast tracts of land, drove in herds of cattle from Texas, and ranged them on the plentiful grass.

For the first two decades the winters were open and cattle foraged year around. Hay was put up only for saddle horses and barnyard stock. Then came the summer of 1888 and one of the worst droughts on record. Waterholes dried up. Many cattle died and those that survived went into winter in terrible condition. A mild winter would have been hard on the stock but this winter was like no other in history.

In November the first storm swept down from the Arctic. Over the next four months storm after storm, bringing freezing cold and snow, surged across the West. At first cattle were able to paw through the ice crust, scraping skin and flesh from their legs, to reach the grass beneath. As winter dragged on they turned to stripping bark from willows along the streams to survive, and as a last resort they chewed on each other's manes and tails. Cattle died by the tens of thousands.

The devastating winter was known as the "Great Equalizer". Ranchers went broke. Some attempted to rebuild from scratch. Others never even tried. They knew the era of the cattle baron was over.

THE TRADE

This is a tale of a buckaroo who decided to settle down. He opened a trading post.

One day an Indian stopped and asked if the trader were interested in selling a fine-looking pinto tied to the hitching rail out front. "Might be," the trader told him. For the next half hour the two haggled over the price.

At last a deal was struck. The Indian paid and galloped away on the horse. The trader stood in front of the window watching and, when the windbroken horse pulled up half a mile away because he could run no farther, the trader let out a belly laugh. He had fooled the Indian. He had got the best of the trade.

Some time later the Indian and several members of his tribe arrived at the trading post. The owner sensed trouble but the Indians were friendly and at last the white man concluded the previous trade had been forgotten.

One of the Indians was riding a bay horse with excellent conformation. The trader asked if it was for sale. The Indian shook his head no. This refusal only piqued the trader's interest and made him more determined. Finally he offered to race one of his horses against the bay, winner take all. The Indians held a quick council and agreed to the terms if the race would be from the trading post, around a lone juniper tree and back. The distance was slightly more than a quarter mile.

The bay won the race going away and, of course, the trader insisted on buying the Indian horse. He knew several buckaroos who would pay top dollar for the animal. Eventually the Indians agreed to swap and they quickly departed with the trader's best horse and a new rifle.

The trader gave the bay a close inspection and recognized something. A bucket of water and some elbow grease revealed the horse was the windbroken pinto under a coat of brown dye.

SHEEP SHOOTERS

It was a pastoral scene, warm spring rain painting the high desert with soft hues and a large band of sheep wandering over the landscape nibbling on shoots of fresh grass.

The herder was at his campfire pouring another cup of coffee when one of his dogs perked its ears and barked. The herder turned and, skylined on the low rolling hill, he saw eleven riders. The quiet was shattered by the pounding of horses' hooves as the eleven raced into camp. Their faces were blackened to hide identities. They were armed to the teeth with rifles, pistols and clubs.

"Grab a handful of sky," the herder was told in no uncertain terms and he quickly complied. They dragged him over to a scrub juniper, tied him to it and shoved a sack over his head.

It was just as well he did not witness what transpired next, although the sounds were unmistakable -- gunshots popping rhythmically, sheep bleating, dogs barking.

For the eleven strangers it was like a party in a shooting gallery. The sheep scattered and the men continued firing rifles until the sheep were out of range. Then they rode after them, running down small bunches and firing pistols, or leaning low in the saddle and swinging clubs at individual animals.

And then it grew quiet again, very quiet. The herder worked himself free, pulled the bag off his head. A grisly sight lay before him -- dead and dying sheep everywhere.

What happened that day in 1903 near eastern Oregon's Benjamin Lake, was the worst sheep slaughter in the history of the high desert. A total of 2,400 sheep were killed. And for years after, the bleached bones lay as mute testimony to the war waged between cattlemen and sheepmen for supremacy on the desert grasslands.

BLACK DEMON

Dick Stanley was a world champion bronc rider. And when his days as an active performer were drawing to a close, he put together a wild west show and traveled to small towns throughout the West. The star attraction of every show was a jet black horse known far and wide as Black Demon.

The show had cowboys and Indians, trick ropers and trick riders. At the finale Black Demon, all fire and fury, would be led into the arena and Stanley would call out, "This is the meanest outlaw, the worst buckin' bronc in existence. He'll poke a hole in the wind and move faster 'n gossip at a church social. When he gets to poppin' leather, really gets with it, takes fifteen minutes for his shadow to catch up with 'im."

Showman Stanley would paint a formidable picture of Black Demon and then throw out the challenge to "any red-blooded bronc rider", offering $50 cash to the man who could ride Black Demon.

Usually one or maybe two confident cowboys would step over the rail and saunter into the arena. And before their families and friends Black Demon would humble them.

Stanley took the show south. During a performance in California he could not interest even a single volunteer into attempting to ride Black Demon. He chided the men, asking if there were not one man with "guts". But still no one stepped forward.

"All right," announced Stanley. "I'll have a go at him myself."

The blindfold was removed. The snubbing horse cast away. Stanley sat deep in the saddle. Black Demon exploded. He reared, went up and over, thrashed at the sky with all four feet, struggled to stand and ran away.

Stanley lay on the ground, motionless. He was dead.

CATTLE KING

Ben Snipes was born in North Carolina in 1835, came west in 1852 and put together a great cattle empire which stretched from central Oregon north to the Canadian border and from the Cascade Mountains east toward the Rockies.

He built a herd of cattle numbering into the tens of thousands -- even Ben never knew exactly how many cattle he owned -- and drove the bunchgrass-fattened stock north over the Caribou Trail to mining camps in British Columbia.

He was the Cattle King until the terrible winter of 1861-62 which brought one snow storm after another, followed by freezing rain and bitter cold. It took a heavy toll; it was estimated ninety percent of the cattle carrying Snipes's S brand died.

Ben is reported to have said, "They call me Cattle King. Well, I've very likely got more dead cattle than any man in the world, but I'm still a very live cattleman. I have cattle. They're skinny and weak. Many may yet die, but some will live. I accumulated more cattle than all the rest, and I can do as well again."

Ben rebuilt his herd by buying all the cattle he could get his hands on. He returned to his former greatness and in the ensuing years survived other bad winters, floods, rustlers and pilfering by Indians. In the end he was brought down by the financial panic of 1893 which resulted in banks closing and cattle prices dropping to the point where there was no market.

Once again the aging Cattle King made a run. In the fall of 1903 Ben was seen on a back road riding a cayuse pony and leading a single cow. He met one of his former cowboys and told him, "I'm starting in the cattle business again."

Within three years Ben had parlayed his single cow into a small ranch near The Dalles with more than a hundred head. But time ran out for the Cattle King. He died January 12, 1906.

COW CATCHER

The fall of 1892 three cowboys were driving a small herd of fat steers off the open range to the railroad stockyard at Pendleton. They followed the bottomland along the winding Umatilla River where the grass was still green, taking their time, not pushing the animals unnecessarily.

Their last evening on the trail one of the cowboys rode on ahead to find a pasture where they could hold the herd overnight. A farmer told him, "You can use the forty down the lane, it lays alongside the railroad track. Fence should be okay, but if I was you, I'd check it 'fore I turned 'em loose."

The cowboy had every intention of riding the fence line but the herd was already in sight so he opened the gate and helped turn the cattle down the lane and into the pasture. Afterwards the cowboys started a fire, boiled coffee, cooked dinner and relaxed.

The night was dark, only pinpoints of starlight splashed across the black sky, as the cowboys turned in. They were warm and snug in their bedrolls when the ground gave a slight shake, a vibration that was the first sign of an approaching train. Then a far away whoo-whooing began to seep into the cowboys' consciousness. The one who had failed to ride the fence sat straight up. An image raced through his mind of the downed fence. He could see it down. See the fat steers finding it and stepping over the wires, stepping onto the track. He held his breath.

The engine was nearing the trestle over the Umatilla River. The headlight, an all-powerful eye, searched the track ahead. And when the engineer spotted cattle bunched on the track he threw on the brake. Sparks flew. Metal screeched against metal. He pulled the steam whistle. But it was to no avail. The cattle remained on the track.

The cowcatcher cut a swath through the herd and the train continued on, receding into the night. The cowboys discovered nine steers had been killed outright and another seven were so badly injured they had to be destroyed.

ESCAPE TO HORSE HEAVEN

Word was passed around Arlington that a government horse buyer was coming to town and would be paying top dollar for cavalry remounts. A buckaroo by the name of Highfill heard the news, caught the next ferry across the Columbia River and headed north into the Horse Heaven Hills to do some mustanging.

Over the course of the next several days Highfill was able to locate and capture a herd of mustangs led by a fiery buckskin stud. He worked with the stud until the animal would allow himself to be led. Then they started south, Highfill leading the stud and the band following.

They reached the small ferry without incident. Realizing it would take several trips to get his herd across the river, Highfill decided it would be easiest to take the stud with the first bunch.

As the ferry touched the Oregon shore the stallion expelled a high-pitched squeal, reared and leaped into the cold river. The other horses followed. The mustangs swam tightly bunched until the strong current caught them and started to string them out. People gathered on the bluff above to watch Highfill's misfortune.

Near midstream a few of the weaker animals became disoriented and swam in circles trying, it seemed, to determine which bank was closest. The stud returned to them, got their attention and set a straight course for Washington. All the horses fell in line behind their leader except for one old mare who gave up and quit swimming; she floated over on her back and allowed the current to carry her away.

After being in the frigid water for twenty minutes and covering a distance of well over a mile, the buckskin stud pulled himself ashore. He called encouragement to the horses still swimming. After they were recovered from the ordeal he drove them, at a trot, toward the Horse Heaven Hills.

41

THE LONG TRAIL

Richard Helm came over the Oregon Trail with his parents in 1845. When he was of age to attend college he enrolled at Willamette University.

"After attending the university for three years my father told me to take up Hebrew as he wanted me to be able to read the Bible in its original form," recalled Helm. "He planned for me to be a preacher. This scared me out. I didn't want to preach so I stopped school, loaded some grub and tools on a pack horse, mounted my riding horse and started east. I was at Boise when the first tents were put up there.

"In the spring of 1863 I drove a herd of cattle to Fort Simcoe and the following year drove 450 head to the Klickitat Valley. I kept them there until the spring and we sold them for $22,000. In 1880 I drove a herd of cattle to Cheyenne, Wyoming for shipment to eastern markets.

"For 37 years I bought and sold cattle. Much of that time my saddle was my pillow and the sky was my cover. I was like the nomads of old. I had no settled habitation.

"I have never touched a drop of intoxicating liquor in my life. I have never tasted tobacco in any form. Up to 60 years ago I used to drink coffee, but decided to get along without it and have never tasted coffee since.

"I will tell you a rather remarkable thing about my outdoor life. I have gone for days when trailing cattle with my clothes wringing wet, have slept in wet blankets, have forded swollen streams and, although I am 85 years of age, I have never yet had occasion to visit a doctor."

STOCKMAN'S PARADISE

At the turn of the century Bill Brown controlled 38,000 acres of land, 22,000 head of sheep and 12,000 horses.

Brown, a native of Wisconsin, came west in 1869 searching for rangeland and was attracted to the open country of central Oregon. He built his empire by acquiring a section here, a forty there, consolidating his holdings around springs and streams and relying on the government land between to carry his ever-increasing herds.

It was during the first world war that Brown was at his peak. The United States, Canada and France came to the high desert to purchase the hardy mustangs for cavalry remounts. Geldings brought $100 a head and mares $95. In one sale Brown sold more than 1,000 animals.

But the tide turned. The world entered an era of armored warfare and the remount market folded. Brown was reduced to selling his horses to packing plants.

Brown, fighting to hold the land, was once forced to kill a man. The duel in the sage occurred with William Overstreet and involved control of a spring. The two men stepped off nine paces in opposite directions, turned and fired.

Overstreet's death played heavily on Brown's mind and he was never the same man after the shooting. In later years, although he spoke about marrying and rearing a family that would "be a credit to the human race", he remained a bachelor. Homesteaders flooded into the country. They divided up the range, laying claim to springs, streams and access roads and taking their claims to court. They were like a pack of wolves, continually biting at Brown's flank. While he was preoccupied with them, the government launched a two-pronged attack: instituting the Taylor Grazing Act and assessing taxes. Brown was forced to sell chunks of land to pay the money the government said he owed.

Bill Brown died penniless at the age of 86 in a nursing home in Salem, a home he had endowed in his heyday.

HARD TIMES

Jim Bamberry was a product of the depression era.

"During the hard times I took whatever job came along," recalls Jim. "Mostly I roamed from Canada to the Mexican border shearing sheep. A lot of the ranchers and farmers couldn't pay in cash so they would give you wool, meat, feed you and put you up, or if you were lucky they would give you something you could take down the road and sell for a couple bucks.

"When I was a young man I was moving furniture down a steep crooked old stairway and accidentally fell. It banged me up but I never really thought about any long-lasting effect until after I had been shearing for several years. It got to the point where at the end of a day I ached all over -- legs, shoulders, back. Doctor said it was arthritis from when I got knocked down the stairs.

"Along came World War II and I enlisted in the Army but after a couple weeks they mustered me out on account of the arthritis. So I went home to the high desert, worked part time on a ranch and had a sideline buying and selling cattle and calves. Did that for several years before I could afford to pick up a small piece of property. It gave me a base to work from and I added to it whenever a good deal presented itself or whenever cattle were paying.

"Over the years I built my little spread into a ranch. Raised cattle. Rode horseback every day, enjoyed the wide open spaces, was living life just like I wanted.

"But my arthritis got worse and worse and finally it was just too painful for me to ride. It was a terrible realization. If I couldn't ride, I couldn't tend cattle. I sold my horse and started selling a few head of cattle at a time. It would have been too hard to sell them all at once.

"Then one mornin' I woke up and I didn't have cow one to my name. So I whistled for my stock dog, took down my fishing pole, blew off the dust, and went fishing."

MUSTANGING

Jerry Miller ranches on the high desert. He recalls a time when mustanging was a normal practice, before the government became involved and created laws protecting the wild horses.

"I started mustanging when I was about nine," says Jerry. "My brother and I used to go up in the hills and collect horses to break and train for haying. You needed horses on the mowing machines, pulling wagons, loading and stacking.

"Once the hay was put up we would gather horses to sell. One year we collected a thousand head. You can imagine some were pretty wild, had never seen a man before. We rode everything we brought in, or I should say we tried to ride everything we brought in. The real outlaws we hung onto, kept them in our own private bucking string.

"We herded mustangs horseback and trapped them at waterholes. But the best success we had was herding them with airplanes.

"The first pilot on the high desert that I recall was Ted Barber. He had a real knack for being able to slow his plane but still be able to stay in the air, and get behind a herd and drive them the direction he wanted them to go. Sometimes, to get his speed down, we would have to tie on chains, cans, anything we could find to act as a drag.

"I remember this one time Ted was driving a bunch of mustangs toward a trap. He had a cowboy name of Bailey with him. The stud horse in the little band was real wild. Whenever they got him near the trap he would veer away and take the mares with him. This happened several times. Finally Bailey got tired of this routine and the next pass he managed to drop a loop over the head of the stud. You can imagine what happened.

"In the end Bailey claimed he was thinking awful serious about taking another dally and holding on but Ted yelled at him they were going down. Finally it registered, it was better to lose a rope and a horse than his life. He let go."

TRUE CHAMPION

Many of the early-day cowboys were former slaves, freed by the Civil War, who came west to start a new life. One of the best black riders was George Fletcher.

At the Pendleton Round-Up of 1911 George rode in the finals against Jackson Sundown, a Nez Perce Indian, and a white man, John Spain. The horse Sundown drew bumped into a judge's mount and the Indian got behind, lost his balance, was thrown and disqualified.

Spain drew Long Tom, a big sorrel that distinguished himself with a habit, when released from the snubbing horse, of throwing down his head and jerking the rider forward. Long Tom's next move was to stop suddenly and explode straight up. This maneuver would unseat most riders. It was at this point that Spain appeared to grab leather and when the judges did not disqualify him, the crowd booed.

Fletcher drew a horse named Hot Foot that lived up to its name. Fletcher rode him expertly and the crowd roared in response to his loose, fluid style. It was said he looked like a rubber band nailed to a stick.

There seemed to be no doubt in the crowd's mind who had won, but the judges went into conference for several minutes and then announced that John Spain had been awarded the championship. The crowd bellowed in unison, "No! No! No!" and called George Fletcher's name.

The judges' decision caused a controversy that continues to this day. It was said that they discriminated and refused to name a Negro as champion.

Although Fletcher was never given the championship he was mobbed, his shirt torn into strips and distributed to admirers who paid five dollars apiece. Fletcher received several times more money for losing than did Spain for winning.

OUTLAW

Al Jennings was a buckaroo working long cattle drives from Texas to the railroad towns in Kansas and Missouri until the day a lawman killed his brother. After that Al Jennings embarked on a career of holding up stages and robbing trains.

Mrs. Durkee, a homesteader on the plains, recalled her meeting with the notorious Al Jennings. "It was back in the 1890s, a hot summer day with heat shimmering and here and there whirlwinds twisting loose dirt into the sky," she said.

"I first saw him a long way out, him afoot making his way toward our cabin. My husband was gone away to town for several days getting supplies and I was alone with two small children, one a babe in my arms. I could only speculate on the circumstances that would cause a man to be afoot in this land of great distances.

"At last he arrived and stood in the shade of the porch. He was a tall man, slender with a kindly expression in his eyes. He told me, 'Ma'am, I need to borrow a horse.' We had only one saddle horse on the place. He continued, 'I'll take good care of him, not ride him too hard, nor too far. And I'll send him back to you safe and sound.'

"As payment he offered to leave his gold watch with me. How could I refuse? After he departed, riding our horse, I looked at the watch and noticed the name Al Jennings engraved on the back of the case. It gave me quite a start to discover the stranger was a wanted criminal.

"The following day a settler who lived west of us returned our horse and the morning after that my husband arrived, weary from long hours in the saddle. He said he had ridden as fast as he could, telling me, 'A train was robbed near Dodge City and the sheriff believed Al Jennings and his gang were responsible and might be headed in this direction.'

"That's the story of my chance meeting with Al Jennings. I understand he kept running until he reached a place where no one knew him. I was told he changed his ways and became a successful evangelist out in the Northwest."

KILLING OF PETE FRENCH

Pete French arrived on the high desert in 1872 laying claim to the Steens Mountains, the Donner und Blitzen River and its open marshes and meadows and the surrounding sagebrush flats. He established his headquarters at Frenchglen; from there he controlled a ranch extending for hundreds of square miles and including tens of thousands of cattle.

For three long decades Pete French controlled the vast P Ranch empire; fighting Indians, rustlers, squatters, enduring fluctuations in market prices, depressions and financial panics as well as wild swings in weather from blizzards to droughts. He was tough and resilient.

Barbed wire was introduced in 1874 and it forever changed the face of the range. Settlers arrived in the valley of the Donner und Blitzen claiming free homestead land, fencing off the water and the grassy meadows. Pete French and his cowboys tried to hold back the onslaught but it was like trying to hold back a changing tide.

The day after Christmas 1896, homesteader Ed Oliver met Pete French at a closed gate and after a short but heated argument over ownership of the land, he pulled a pistol and gunned down the cattle baron.

Oliver stood trial in Burns. His attorney was L.R. Webster from Portland, a man skilled in matters of law and an elocutionist adept at influencing a jury. He had Mrs. Oliver and her three children, ranging in age from eight years to six months, sit in the first row during the three-day trial. At every opportunity he would stand near them, drawing attention to them. He drummed into the jury's thinking that above all else, Ed Oliver was a family man.

The jury, composed mostly of homesteaders, returned a verdict of "not guilty". Ed Oliver became a free man.

Not long after his release, and without saying anything to anyone, he left the country. It was said he ran off with another woman. A fellow by the name of P.C. Peterson, a homesteader, married Mrs. Oliver and raised the children.

REFLECTIONS

Bill Hanley was one of the most respected ranchers in the West. He spent years trying to bring in the railroad, but when it finally arrived he questioned if he had done the right thing.

In his book *Feelin' Fine*, Hanley wrote, "Had our big railroad celebration. A trainload came from the outside to help us rejoice. All were happy, big speeches and everything.... A fellow builds a railroad across the Plains and we say, 'What a wonderful thing!' But what is he to the Fellow that made the Plains?

"Had to get off my horse and go stand on the rails all alone. Seemed like a mighty lonesome meeting -- all my feeling was of the past. Had worked so much at different times to bring in the steel rails, and here they were. They had followed the old trail we drove cattle over so many times through so many years....

"I thought of the big outfits, the saddle horses, the herds -- how they'd had to move hundreds of miles, living off the country as they went, the many camps, and the many years necessary to learn the skill in handling and moving them. No human would ever be raised again who could know how to do it. No reason ever again why he should. The rails had taken the romance and fascination out of the life of a cattleman.... Anyone can raise cattle and load them into cars.

"They'll be changing our old names that tell people the whole history of the country: Squaw Flats, Yainax, Bake Oven, Rawhide, Stinking Water, Crooked River, Iron Mountain, Desolation Creek, Wagontire, Poison Creek, Wild Horse, Summer Lake, Goose Lake, Happy Valley, Diamond ... so many others, given by the boys, often for things that happened there. All mean something. Every one a story."

FLYING MUSTANGER

"A good pilot can move a band of mustangs 20 miles and never get a hair wet. That's the way it's supposed to be done," claimed Frank Stinton who was a mustanging pilot back in the 1930s.

"The secret is to stay back. You never made a pass directly over them. What you try to do is stay behind cutting figure eights back and forth, and gently push them the direction you want them to go.

"Horses handle better in bunches of eight or ten. One time I brought in 18 head but that was nothing but blind luck. You pick out a stud and a few mares, take them to the trap and circle back for more. I would work an area all day and maybe have between 50 and 150 head in the corral by the time the sun set.

"To be a flying mustanger you didn't necessarily have to be an aerobatic pilot, but you did have to be able to catch updrafts and ride air currents because planes of that vintage had gas tanks that only gave you a couple hours in the air. The best description I can think of to describe that type of flying is to say it was by the seat of your pants."

At the zenith of Frank's flying career he was unexpectedly grounded. A strong, active man of 37, he contracted polio and in a matter of a few weeks he was paralyzed. He spent a month in an iron lung. Doctors told him if he had delayed coming to the hospital by even a day the polio would have killed him.

"The hardest adjustment was realizing I would never be able to pilot another plane, that I would never mustang again," said Frank. "From time to time friends around McDermitt take me up in their planes. And when they do, I'm constantly searching the horizon for the telltale signs of dust that mean wild horses are on the move."

RECORD MARE

Paddy never knew the wide open spaces of the high desert, driving cattle across the alkali flats, smelling the sweet tang of sage after a rainstorm. She was foaled on the west side of the mountains, in rural Willamette Valley on the farm of W.G. Walker.

Walker was a pioneer of 1852. He homesteaded near St.Paul and was content farming until 1905 when he was awarded a mail contract. He used Paddy to pull his buggy on a 30-mile-a-day route through the country. In summer the roads were dry and dusty; rain would turn them to a muddy bog. In any weather, Paddy diligently went about her job, learning the route, stopping at mailboxes as she came to them.

Paddy was a sorrel, a white star on her forehead being her most identifiable marking. She was alert, spirited, but in no way spooky. Tumbleweeds could blow across the path, pheasants could rise up squawking from the grass beside the road. Paddy would ignore all distractions. She was steady and strong.

At the turn of the century rural residents ordered most of their goods from catalogs and some days the mail buggy would be filled to overflowing with personal mail, packaged clothing and machinery, sometimes packaged and sometimes not. If a postal patron were in dire need of medicine or groceries and left a note to that effect in the mailbox, Walker would, the following day, deliver what was needed.

For thirteen years Walker was responsible for delivering the mail. When he retired Paddy was turned out to pasture. In her tenure as a mail carrier the faithful Paddy logged over 75,550 miles -- the equivalent of three trips around the world.

WAR HORSE

The Modoc tribe withdrew from the reservation they shared with the Klamath Indians. The ensuing war became the bloodiest in the history of the Northwest, costing the lives of 41 soldiers, including seven commissioned officers, and all but decimating the Modoc tribe.

During the final battle of the Lava Beds the Indians retreated and the soldiers overran their position. According to Captain Harrison Kelley, commander of a company of militia from Jacksonville, Oregon, "The Indians abandoned their horses and my men, using every rope available and even tearing shirts into strips and tying the ends together, captured as many of the ponies as they could even though I told them they were foolish, that the ponies weren't worth the bother. It had been my experience that Indian ponies were underfed and overworked. Consequently, they did not make good mounts.

"After we returned to Jacksonville, one of the men brought me an Indian pony and offered to sell it to me for thirty-five dollars. The horse was spotted, had a roached mane and was in remarkably good condition. I paid the thirty-five dollars; took to calling my little pony by the name Billy."

Billy was surefooted, could cut cattle and possessed outstanding endurance. On several occasions Captain Kelley covered more than 60 miles in a single day while riding Billy.

In 1905 Captain Kelley gave a Paiute Indian permission to ride Billy in the Lewis and Clark Exposition parade in Portland. Afterward the old war horse was turned out to pasture. He lived to be more than forty years old.

COWBOY HAT

The cowboy is an individualist who outfits himself according to his personality. It is not unusual to see a Nevada buckaroo wearing Mexican spurs, Plains chaps, Texas boots and riding an Oregon Hamley saddle over an Indian blanket. But the most integral part of his outfit is his hat.

John Batterson Stetson came out with a high-crowned, curled brim hat he called the "Plainsman" in the 1870s. Cowboys found it the perfect hat. The rounded crown furnishes an air space over the heat on hot days and no place for rain to gather on wet days. The brims are dipped slightly in front and back allowing water to run off and the sides are curled so they do not catch the wind.

Many stories attest to the durability of the Stetson. One has it that two holdup men were hung at Weeksville, Montana in 1882 and buried with their Stetsons. When the remains were exhumed 42 years later, the hats were still recognizable.

Another story tells of a man trapped by fire. He dug a trench and buried himself with dirt except for his face which he covered snug with his Stetson. The hat came through the fire still holding its shape but charred coal black. It served its purpose.

A cowboy might spend a month's wages to buy a new hat but never wants it to have that just-out-of-the-box look. On his way out the door of the western wear store, he likely will be working to shape it. He may punch it, twist it or knock a few dents in the crown. He might toss it in the dirt a time or two. Finally, when sweat has stained the crown and rugged use and constant tugging have shaped the brim, then and only then does the hat fit.

TEBO

Tebo was a buckaroo who loved to tell a good story.

One evening after working cattle all day, the buckaroos gathered around the fire drinking coffee and smoking hand-rolled cigarettes. Tebo was sitting on his haunches talking to a cattle buyer from Portland. He asked the man if he had ever been into the Steens.

"Just to the foothills. Never actually into the mountains. From what I hear, they're awful rugged," said the buyer.

"They are," confirmed Tebo. He took a drink of strong coffee and continued. "If you ever get up there be sure to see Kiger Gorge. It's a sight. Sides straight up, straight down.

"One time I was ridin' up there for cattle. I climbed to the top and by then my horse was pretty well spent. While I was waiting for him to get his wind I noticed this big boulder perched on the very edge. I could see it wouldn't take much to upset the delicate balance and send it over the rim.

"Like I said, I was just killin' time anyway so I ambled over and put my shoulder into the boulder. It didn't take much. I give a shove and jumped back quick. It teetered there for a second and went. I watched as it crashed and banged, going downhill, picking up speed."

Tebo was quiet for a moment, rolling and lighting a cigarette, allowing the cattle buyer to build a mental picture of that boulder bouncing higher and higher every time it hit. Finally the cattle buyer asked, "Is that it?"

"Hell no," answered Tebo. "Just give me a minute." He poured coffee all around the circle of buckaroos and refilled the cattle buyer's cup before continuing.

"The next spring I was back up in Kiger and would you believe that my rock was still rolling back and forth, from one side of the gorge to the other. But by then it was only about this big around." He held his hand about a foot apart.

56

BRANDED

Alex Zevely was an old man when he related the following story, "I grew up along the Klamath River and started school at Keno, Oregon.

"I was the smallest boy in school. Dan Doten was the biggest. Somewhere I got a picture of him and he was half a head taller than the teacher.

"Dan was always playing he was a buckaroo. One recess he talked me into being a mustang. I was supposed to act wild. Dan and some of the other boys chased me. I led them down by the barn, dodging the loops they threw, pawing the air, acting like the rankest mustang in the West.

"They finally caught me and threw me to the ground. I played along, whinnying, kicking and biting at them. And when they had me tied so I couldn't move, Dan got the bright idea they should brand me. While one of them fetched a few forks of loose hay and started a fire Dan found a piece of wire and formed one end into DD, his initials.

"I didn't really think they would carry it out, not until someone peeled down my britches and Dan laid the red-hot wire on my left hip. I let out a scream that would curl the whiskers on a mountain lion. The boys ran away, left me tied with fire creeping toward the barn full of hay.

"I yelled and yelled and finally a passerby heard me, put the fire out and untied me. I ran home and Mother put wormwood salve on the burn.

"Lot of years have come and gone. Water under the bridge. I still have a trace of the brand on my hip, looks like I'll carry it to my grave.

"Even after the branding I always looked up to Dan. I understand they've got him over to the old folk's home in Klamath Falls now, but I'll bet he remembers. If you went over and asked him about branding me I know what he would do -- laugh."

57

COWBOY WAY

A real cowboy shows the fact in the way he sits a horse. You can see it in his eyes, the tilt of his hat, the swagger in his walk.

Cowboys need only enough money to get by. If they do have a few extra dollars they get rid of it and buy a silk bandanna, chaps, boots, go to a dance, drink it up. They treasure their freedom above material wealth.

You never hear of cowboys wanting to form a labor union, striking for higher wages or hiring a business manager to handle their private affairs. They work under the rules of a particular outfit boss and when the rules do not fit, they pull up stakes and head down the road to the next ranch.

You never hear a cowboy talking about being stuck in a rut, driving time, parking problems, social security, retirement, licenses, permits, registrations. A cowboy does not worry about whether a politician will keep his promises or whether a rainstorm will ruin the family's camping trip. He takes whatever the world and Mother Nature deal out.

As a cowboy rides the range he tends to accumulate things, things like loneliness, fatigue, droughts, storms and the aches and pains from everyday life. He saves them up, goes to town and breaks loose -- fighting, drinking and enjoying the company of a woman, but avoiding marriage because "women always try to tie you down."

In this civilized day and age we have rodeos, dude ranches, books, magazines, television specials and movies dedicated to the cowboy. But being a cowboy is not something you see in an arena or on the printed page or the screen. It is something that grows from within. It is a way of life.